Financial Reality Check

Personal Finance and Budgeting Workbook for Beginner/Teens

Financial Reality Check by Robyn Joyner

First Published Edition: September 2023

Independently published via Kindle Direct Publishing

ISBN: 9798858290377

Copyright © 2023 by Robyn Joyner

Other Curriculum by Robyn Joyner

Teen Financial Reality Fair: Planning Toolkit
Learning Cursive in Narnia
Learning Cursive with The Hobbit
Learning Cursive with Anne of Green Gables
Learning Cursive with Proverbs
Learning Cursive with Charlotte's Web
Learning Cursive with Aesop's Fables
Writing in the Wardrobe: Narnia Print Workbook
Writing God's Word on Your Heart: Proverbs Print Workbook
Writing with Charlotte's Web: Print Workbook
Writing with Aesop's Fables: Print Workbook

INDEX

Income and Careers

- Identify how career choice, education, skills, entrepreneurship, and unexpected life events affect income.
- Identify the effects of tax bracket, gross versus net income, and employee health benefits.

Planning and Managing Money

- Identify the difference between needs and wants when making financial decisions.
- Demonstrate responsibility for personal financial decisions with the use of a Monthly Budget Tracker.
- Gain awareness of debt on a monthly budget.
- Identify the relationship between spending practices and achieving financial goals.

Savings and Investing

- Understand the importance of saving money on a regular basis.
- Explain the relationship between saving practices and reaching financial goals.
- Devise an investment plan for accumulating money for retirement.
- Determine how charitable giving can fit into a personal budget and appropriate percentages for giving.

Individual Chapter Objectives

There is no way to prepare students for every financial decision they will have to make in their adulthood, but we have isolated key learning objectives in each Expense Chapter that will aid your student in their future financial decisions.

Housing

- All housing options have additional costs in addition to monthly rent or mortgage.
- Buying can result in cheaper monthly payments and allow you to create equity but can include more unexpected costs.
- Renting is usually more expensive monthly, but typically has lower unexpected costs.
- Living at home is not free.

Transportation

- Owning a vehicle has hidden costs on top of monthly payments.

- When considering buying a vehicle you must factor in car maintenance, insurance, and gas must into overall cost assessment.

Health
- Health insurance is complicated and varies greatly depending on your needs.
- Health Insurance is typically less expensive if an employer provides it.
- Lower monthly premiums mean higher deductibles.

Food
- Budgeting for food involves factoring in groceries plus any take-out, restaurants, or drinks.

Electronics
- Relying solely on free Wi-Fi may not be possible in the modern world.
- The cost of cell phones can vary greatly.

Personal Care
- Cost of personal items, such as clothing, grooming, and home goods, can add up quickly in a monthly budget.
- Your clothing budget should match your career choice.

Entertainment
- Subscription and entertainment costs add up quickly.
- Vacations are expensive and should be budgeted for ahead of time.
- Pet needs, including veterinarian visits, must be budgeted for.

Education
- In general, the more education you have the higher your overall wages will be depending on what you study.
- Higher education and professional training are not free.
- The cost of colleges varies greatly based on private versus public.
- When choosing a college, consider your return on investment.

Savings
- Start saving early for retirement.
- Make a savings plan that allows you to achieve life goals.
- Factor in charitable giving.
- Christmas and birthdays are not an unexpected event and should be budgeted for monthly.

Junior high and high school students will have the opportunity to encounter some of the financial challenges they will face as an adult, such as the cost of housing, entertainment, and transportation. This is a lesson in balancing wants and needs within the constraints of their monthly income.

Spend time after each chapter talking to your student about what they learned. Use that time to share your own experiences with personal finance and answer any questions they may have.

Questions you can ask after each spending chapter:
1. What choices were hard to make, and which were easy?
2. What information was new to you in this spending chapter?
3. Has this chapter changed your view on spending? If so, how?

Grading

When your student has completed their Monthly Budget Tracker, you will initial to verify the student has visited each budgeting item on their Budget Tracker. If they chose to have a roommate to lower housing costs, check to see if they have listed a specific name of someone they know and contacted.

Students will end their budget practice by balancing their budget. The goal is to successfully complete and balance their budget to a zero sum. Check their math and initial if they have not spent more or less than their monthly income.

- *If student spends more than their monthly income* they will need to revisit earlier chapters and make different spending choices, which is why we encourage using pencil. This budget does not include personal loans or debt options if the student overspends.
- *If the student spends less than their income money* at the end of their monthly budget, encourage them to revisit the *Savings* chapter. Setting aside savings for specific goals and retirement is an important lesson for young adults.

Optional- Local Cost of Living Budget

The salaries and prices in this book are based on living in the most populated areas of the United States, the South and the Midwest. After your student has completed their first practice budget using predetermined prices & salaries, they will have the opportunity to complete another Monthly Budget Tracker using local entry level salaries and local cost of living. This is an optional exercise and will need more assistance from you as their teacher. The students can use some of the predetermined costs in the earlier chapters, but they will need to identify their *local* salaries and cost of living. They can do that by:

1. Internet research. Internet Resources for Local Prices can be found on *Page 71* of this workbook.
2. Asking friends and family their costs of living

Suggested Schedule

WEEK	Day 1	Day 2	Day 3	Day 4
1	**Unit 1-** Pg 9-11 Career Survey, Pick a Job	Pg 15-16 Income Planning & Taxes Worksheet	**Unit 2-** Pg 19 Bank and Budget Tracker	Pg 20-25 Housing
2	Pg 26-29 Food	Pg 30-34 Transportation	Page 35-38 Health Insurance	Pg 39-42 Electronics
3	Pg 43-47 Personal Care	Pg 48-51 Education	Pg 52-57 Savings	Pg 58-62 Entertainment
4	Pg 63 Chance Pg 65-Balance Your Budget	Pg 66-67 Student Reflection	Pg 68-70- Local Cost of Living	Pg 68-70- Local Cost of Living (cont)

Suggested Homeschool Cooperative Schedule

WEEK	
1	**Unit 1**- Pg 9-11 Career Survey, Pick a Job
2	Pg 15-16 Income Planning & Taxes Worksheet
3	**Unit 2**- Pg 19 Bank and Budget Tracker & Pg 20-25 Housing
4	Pg 26-29 Food & Pg 30-34 Transportation
5	Pg 35-38 Health Insurance & Pg 39-42 Electronics
6	Pg 43-47 Personal Care
7	Pg 48-51 Education
8	Pg 52-57 Savings
9	Pg 58-62 Entertainment & Pg 63 Chance
10	Pg 65 Balance Your Budget (revisit past chapter is needed)
11	Pg 65-67 Student Reflection & Discussion
12	Pg 68-70- Local Cost of Living Research

Unit I:

Career and Income Planning

1. Take a Career Survey

This workbook will be more meaningful if you take the time for self-assessment before picking your career. Your career choice will determine your monthly income, i.e. what you have to spend, but do not make the mistake of picking a job based on salary alone. Take the time to complete a few Career and Personality Quizzes so that you pick an option based on your own strengths and weaknesses. You do not have to use all of these surveys, pick 1 to 3 to complete before moving onto job options.

Free Online Career Surveys
Student Interest Survey for Career Clusters® **https://cte.careertech.org/sites/default/files/StudentInterestSurvey-English.pdf**
Princeton Review Quiz **https://www.princetonreview.com/quiz/career-quiz**
Career Aptitude Test **https://www.123test.com/career-test**
Personality Career Quiz **www.k12.com/stride-career-prep/career-exploration/career-quiz.html**
Your Free Career Test *https://www.yourfreecareertest.com/*

2. Consider education costs and commitment when picking a career

When picking your career from job options, remember to look at the educational requirements, not just the salary. Are you willing to go to school for several years after high school? The costs of a college education will also be a factor when you complete your budget. Your salary is generally higher after receiving a college degree, but your education costs will also be more expensive, and vice versa.

Higher Education Degrees	Post High School Years Needed to Achieve
Certificate	6 months to one year
Associate's	2 years
Bachelor's	4 years
Master's	6 years
Doctorate	8+ years

3. Pick your career from Job Options

The job options in this workbook are not an exhaustive list but will give you an idea of entry level positions in your field of interest. Each job has a yearly salary, *all positions provided are entry level salaries*, none are above $75,000. **You will not enter the working field at the top of the pay scale**.

Pay Scale- A system that determines how much an employee is to be paid, based on one or more factors such as the employee's level, rank or status within the employer's organization, the length of time that the employee has been employed, and the difficulty of the specific work performed.

Entry Level - A job that is normally designed or designated for recent graduates of a given line of work and typically does not require prior experience in the profession. These roles may require some on-site training on top of your degree.

Salary- A fixed regular payment, typically paid on a monthly or biweekly basis but often expressed as an annual amount, made by an employer to an employee. A salaried employee typically works 40 hours a week, but does not receive extra money for hours worked over that time.

Hourly Employee- Hourly employees are paid at a set hourly rate which is multiplied by the hours worked during a pay period.

Benefits- Perks provided to employees in addition to their base salaries and wages, such as healthcare and retirement.

Your first job may be hourly, not salaried, but for simplicity of this exercise all options are entry-level salaried positions. Salary employees earn consistent paychecks regardless of the hours they work, while hourly pay varies by the amount worked in a week.

Job Options

Job Title	Education Needed	Entry-Level Yearly Salary	Health Insurance
Agriculture, Food, & Natural Resources			
Farmer	High School Diploma	$35,000	Marketplace
Landscape Company Employee	High School Diploma	$29,000	Marketplace
Landscape Design Architect	Associate's	$46,000	Marketplace
DNR Conservation Officer	Bachelor's	$42,000	Employer
Architecture & Construction			
House Painter	High School Diploma	$28,000	Marketplace
General Contractor	Associate's	$43,000	Marketplace
Heating and Cooling (HVAC)	Certificate	$46,000	Employer
Architect	Bachelor's	$55,000	Employer
Art, A/V Tech, & Communications			
Artist/Actor	High School Diploma	$18,000	Marketplace
Graphic Designer	Associate's	$35,000	Marketplace
Audio Visual Technician	Associate's	$34,000	Marketplace
Journalist/Writer	Bachelor's	$37,000	Marketplace
Business Management & Administration			
Administrative Assistant	High School Diploma	$29,000	Marketplace
Payroll Specialist	Certificate	$37,000	Marketplace
Human Resources	Bachelor's	$45,000	Employer
Business Administration	Bachelor's	$50,000	Employer

Education and Training			
Day Care Worker/Certified Development Associate (CDA)	Certificate	$24,000	Marketplace
Preschool Teacher	Associate's	$30,000	Marketplace
Elementary or High School Teacher	Bachelor's	$48,000	Employer
College Professor	Master's	$65,000	Employer
Finance			
Bookkeeper	Associate's	$34,000	Marketplace
Accountant	Bachelor's	$46,000	Employer
Financial Advisor	Bachelor's	$52,000	Marketplace
Business Analyst	Bachelor's	$50,000	Employer
Government and Public Administration			
City Clerk Assistant	Associate's	$35,000	Employer
Policy Analyst	Bachelor's	$55,000	Employer
Urban Planner	Master's	$75,000	Employer
Health Science			
Certified Nursing Assistant (CNA)	Certificate	$33,000	Employer
Associate Degree in Nursing (ADN)	Associate's	$50,000	Employer
Bachelor's Registered Nurse (BRN)	Bachelor's	$60,000	Employer
Medical Doctor (M.D)	Doctorate	$150,00	Employer
Hospitality and Tourism			
Restaurant Server	High School Diploma	$25,000	Marketplace
Cosmetologist	Certificate	$30,000	Marketplace

Restaurant Chef/Culinary Arts	Associate's	$33,000	Marketplace
Hospitality Administration	Associate's	$45,000	Employer
Human Services			
Human Services assistant	Associate's	$28,000	Employer
Social Worker/Case Manager	Bachelor's	$33,000	Employer
Community outreach worker	Bachelor's	$33,000	Employer
Counselor	Master's	$60,000	Employer
Information and Technology			
IT Support	Associate's	$55,000	Employer
Cybersecurity	Associate's	$65,000	Employer
Software Development	Associate's	$56,000	Employer
Software Engineer	Bachelor's	$65,000	Employer
Law, Public Safety & Corrections, Security			
Police Officer	High School Diploma	$43,000	Employer
Firefighter/Emergency Medical Technician	Certificate	$42,000	Employer
Parole Officer	Bachelor's	$47,000	Employer
Attorney	Bachelor's + Law School	$75,000	Employer
Manufacturing			
Assembly Line Worker	High School Diploma	$38,000	Employer
Building Maintenance	High School Diploma	$35,000	Marketplace
Mechanic	Certificate	$45,000	Marketplace
Automation & Robotics	Associate's	$54,000	Employer

Marketing			
Customer Service Associate	High School Diploma	$28,000	Marketplace
Digital Marketing Associate	Associate's	$44,000	Marketplace
Junior Marketing Executive	Bachelor's	$50,000	Employer
Science, Technology, Engineering, Mathematics			
Engineer	Bachelor's	$75,000	Employer
Chemist	Bachelor's	$65,000	Employer
Biologist	Bachelor's	$65,000	Employer
Transportation and Distribution			
UPS Driver	High School Diploma	$50,000	Employer
Supply Chain manager	Associate's	$50,000	Employer

Your Choice

Career	
Yearly Salary	
Degree Needed	
Health Benefits	

Record your job option above. Your job choice includes information regarding the education level needed to obtain that position and if health benefits are provided, this data will be needed to complete your monthly budget.

4. Income Planning- Determine your monthly take home pay

You have chosen your job, now you need to determine what your monthly income. Many simply divide their salary by 12 (months in a year) and think that is what they have to spend each month, but that is not the case. Young adults are often surprised that the check they actually receive isn't as much as they thought it would be because they forgot to factor in taxes.

Income- Money received, especially on a regular basis, for work or through investments.

Gross Income- The sum of all wages and earnings before any taxes are taken out.

Net Income/Take-Home Pay- Net income is the gross income minus taxes. Net Income is also known as "take hone pay" because it is what you take home after your employer takes taxes out of your paycheck. If you are self-employed, your check will be whole, but you will have to put aside money to pay taxes later.

Taxes- A mandatory payment or charge collected by local, state, and federal governments from individuals or businesses to cover the costs of general government services, goods, and activities. Taxes pay for government services, like fire departments, road repair, police, and libraries.

The way taxes are collected and used is hotly debated in every state in America, but workbook is not designed for this debate. In this exercise we discuss taxes just to remind you that you need to factor them in when planning your monthly budget. Every state has a different tax system, but every person must factor in federal taxes to their monthly budget.

Income Tax- A mandatory contribution to government revenue, collected by the government on s worker's income.

Federal Income taxes- percentage of money that you pay to the federal government based on the income you make at your job. They are based on your income, not by where you live.

State Income taxes- percentage of money that you pay to the state government based on the income you make at your job, which varies by state.

Tax Bracket- The federal tax rate you will pay on each portion of your income.

You can calculate your taxes by dividing your income into the segments that will be taxed in each applicable bracket. If you make more money, you do not get taxed at a higher rate on ALL your money, only on the amount over that bracket.

On the next page you will estimate how much federal taxes you will have taken out of your paycheck every month. The numbers in the tax bracket are rounded for easier calculations. To convert a percentage decimal, divide by 100 (just move the decimal point 2 places to the left). Then multiply your income by that decimal. Subtract your total taxes from your Yearly Salary to get your Yearly Take-Home Pay. Dive that number by twelve months in a year to determine your monthly income (money you have to spend in a month)

Income Planning & Taxes Worksheet

Occupation:

Yearly Salary (Gross Income):

Education Level Needed:

Yearly Take Home Pay (Net Income):

Divide your income into the segments of the tax bracket. Calculate your taxes using sample below.

Tax bracket (based on Annual Salary)	Tax Rate	Your Income	Taxes
The first $11,000	10%		
The next $11,000 – $45,000	12%		
The next $45,00– $95,000	22%		
The next $95,00– $180,000	24%		
The next $180,000 – $230,000	32%		
The next $230,000 – $575,000	35%		
Over $575,000	37%		
	TOTAL		

SAMPLE *So, if you earn $65,000, your federal taxes will look like this:*

Tax bracket (based on Annual Salary)	Tax Rate	Your Income	Taxes
The first $11,000	10%	$11,000	x .10= $1,100
The next $11,000 to $45,000	12%	$34,000	x .12= $4,080
The next $45,000 to $95,000	22%	$20,000	x .22= $4,400
		$65,000	$9,580 Total Taxes

Subtract Your total taxes from your Yearly Salary to get your Yearly Take-Home Pay

_____ - _____ = _____

Yearly Salary   Total Taxes   Yearly Take-Home Pay

Monthly Net Income (Take Home Pay)

Divide your Yearly Take Home Pay by 12 = _____

Monthly Take Home Pay

(Money you have to spend in a month)

Unit II:

Budget Practice

BEGIN YOUR MONTHLY BUDGET

Adults begin their monthly budget with a visit to the bank, either physically or digitally. Your paycheck may be given to you or be deposited directly into your bank account.

After choosing your job, you will begin filling out your Monthly Budget Tracker. Each chapter will present you with a spending choice regarding an adult's average monthly expenses: housing, food, entertainment, transportation, etc.

Expenses- the cost required for something; the money spent on something.

All expenses in this workbook are based on a one income entry level position, without children. As your expenses grow with age, your income will hopefully grow accordingly.

Balancing Your Budget

Please use a pencil for your monthly budget because you may have to make changes to past choices as you progress through the spending chapters. This budget does not include personal loans or debt options if you overspend. If you run out of money, you will need to revisit a previous chapter and make different spending choices.

Budget- A spending plan based on your income and expenses.

Balanced Budget- When your planned income matches the amount of planned expenses. In short, a balanced budget is when you have successfully not spent or less more than you earned.

When you have completed your Monthly Budget Tracker, your teacher will initial to verify you have completed every spending chapter and not gone over budget. The goal is to successfully complete and balance your budget.

If you have extra money at the end of your monthly budget, revisit the savings chapter. Setting aside savings for specific goals and retirement is an important lesson for your future.

Monthly Budget Tracker

HOUSING

Rent or Mortgage _____

Insurance _____

Utilities _____

Roommate   *Roommate Initials* _____
                  Teacher Initials _____

Housing Total _____

TRANSPORATION

Monthly Payment _____

Car Insurance _____

Gas _____

Auto Repair _____

Bus or Uber _____

Registration _____

Transportation Total _____

FOOD

Groceries _____

Fast Food _____

Take-out _____

Restaurants _____

Coffee/Drinks _____

Food Total _____

HEALTH

Monthly Premium _____

Vision _____

Dental _____

Health Total _____

PERSONAL

Clothing _____

Home Goods _____

Personal Grooming _____

Personal Total _____

EDUCATION

Monthly Payment _____

Education Total _____

Career	
Yearly Salary	
Degree Needed	
Health Benefits	
Monthly Take-Home Pay	

ELECTRONICS

Cell Phone _____

Internet _____

Electronics Total _____

ENTERTAINMENT

Movies & Music _____

Vacation _____

Pet Care _____

Entertainment Total _____

SAVINGS

Retirement _____

Home Repair _____

House Down Payment _____

Save for New Car _____

Gift Fund _____

Give to Charity _____

Saving Total _____

CHANCE

Roll One _____

Roll Two _____

Chance Total _____

END OF MONTH BALANCE: _____

TEACHER INITIALS: _____

HOUSING

Housing Directions

Your first task as an adult is finding a place to live. Choosing a place to live will determine all your other expenses. Your housing choice will depend on your income, what kind of life you would like to live, and personal goals. Your choices are between renting, buying, or living at home. There are advantages and disadvantages to all these options.

RENTING

Most young people start off by renting their first place to live. There are advantages to renting, with less responsibilities than home ownership and more flexibility. Renting also provides more predictable monthly expenses and the landlord is responsible to fix needed repairs.

Landlord- A property owner who rents that property to another party in exchange for rent payments. Landlords can be individuals or businesses.

Tenant- A person who lives on land or in a property rented from a landlord.

Rent- A tenant's regular payment to a landlord for the use of property or land. Most rentals include a contract that agrees upon the time you will live there, generally six months to a year, with an agreement that rent will not rise during that period.

Utilities- Basic services for your home or apartment that are needed to keep it comfortable and functioning properly. Common utilities include water, sewer, electricity, gas, trash, and recycling.

Renting also has disadvantages. If your landlord decides to raise the price on your rental, you must pay more or move when your contract ends. You are not creating long term wealth when you rent. At the end of the rental contract, you do not get your rent money back.

Renter's Insurance- Protects your personal property in a rented apartment, condo, or home from unexpected circumstances such as theft, a fire or water damage.

BUYING

Buying a home comes with many advantages, including being in control of your own living space, home equity and appreciation. Home ownership brings intangible benefits as well, such as a sense of stability and pride of ownership. Owning a home is a long-term investment. You will see some short-term benefits with lower monthly costs than rent, but the long-term financial benefits of owning a home are substantial.

Equity- The value of the possession minus any outstanding debt. When you pay your house loan, you are building home equity. Unlike rent, you get that equity back when you sell your home. The longer you live in a home, the more money you get back when you sell it. When you pay your entire mortgage you'll hold 100% equity in your home and will no longer have monthly payments.

Mortgage - The type of loan typically used to buy a home. If you pay off your Mortgage loan you will no longer have to pay monthly to live in your home because you will own the home. There are different types of mortgages.

Houses always appreciate over time, but it takes patience. The housing market varies on how fast the value of a house appreciates, but the average is 4% every year. If you plan to live in a home for 10 years or more, the statistics of American housing market has proven your home will be worth close to 40% more than what you bought it for.

Appreciation- the increase in the value of a property or asset over time.

Home ownership has long term financial benefits, but it also comes with more responsibility than renting. If something in your home breaks, you are responsible for fixing it. Repairs can be small or can cost thousands of dollars. Utilities can also be more expensive and less predictable in a home.

Homeowner's Insurance- Provides financial coverage to repair or rebuild your home after events like fire, smoke, theft, a falling tree, or damage caused by weather. Most homeowners' insurance also covers furniture, clothing, and other possessions.

Down payment- An initial payment made when something is bought on credit. A down payment is a percentage of your home's purchase price that you pay up front when you close your home loan. Down payments are generally needed to buy a house if you need to use a loan to buy. The bigger your mortgage down payment, the lower your monthly loan payments will be.

Closing costs- Costs you pay when you obtain a mortgage for your home, beyond the down payment costs. Closing costs are commonly 3 to 5 percent of the loan amount and may include title insurance, attorney fees, appraisals, taxes and more.

Interest Rate- if you are a borrower, the interest rate is the amount you are charged for borrowing money, shown as a percentage of the total amount of the loan.

Credit Score- A number between 300–850 that tells how reliable you are at paying bills or any debt. A credit score is based on credit history: number of open accounts, total amount of debt, and repayment history, and other factors.

Credit scores play a significant role in finding housing. Most people cannot afford to buy a home without a mortgage. If you plan to borrow money to buy a home, better credit scores will make it less expensive to buy a house because you will qualify for a lower interest rate. Many landlords will not rent to you or may charge you more per month if your score is too low. A low credit score could keep you from qualifying for a loan at all, be it for a home or a vehicle.

Types of Mortgages

Conventional Loan	A home buyer's loan that is not offered or secured by a government entity. Best for borrowers with a good or excellent credit score.
FHA Loan	First Time Homebuyer (FHA) home loans require lower minimum credit scores and down payments than many conventional loans, which makes them popular with first-time homebuyers.
VA Loan	Home Loan exclusively for military borrowers to buy and refinance homes, guaranteed by the U.S. Department of Veterans Affairs (VA).
USDA Loan	Available for households and/or properties located in designated rural areas that meet all the eligibility requirements

LIVING AT HOME

Living at home still requires you to contribute to the household costs, generally in the form of rent. In this exercise, living at home rent will help your family with their mortgage, utilities, and Wi-Fi. You will have to pay separately for your own groceries in this workbook.

There are benefits to living at home. If you get along with your family, it is also a comfort to have company or help you if you get sick. You can also use the time to save up for another life goal, like a down payment for a home, pay off student loans, or starting your own business.

The disadvantage is you may give up much of your personal freedom and independence in exchange for lower cost of housing. Lack of privacy comes alongside sharing most of your communal spaces with your family. Consider how long you would like to live at home as an adult, then make a plan to save for a house down payment at the savings chapter.

MAKE YOUR HOUSING CHOICE

Roommate: You can lower your cost of renting if you have a roommate but choosing a person to live with is not as easy as it sounds. If you choose the roommate option, you must contact a specific person you know and ask them if they would hypothetically live with you. Your teacher will be checking to see if you have a specific name.

Home Repairs: If you choose to buy a home, you will have to save for home repairs when you get to the Savings Chapter in your Monthly Budget Tracker.

Review the expenses of renting vs. buying, then choose the option you think would work best for you.

BUYING A HOME	Monthly Mortgage+*	Home-owner's Insurance	Utilities
Small Home 2 bedrooms/1 bathroom/900 Sq. Ft $125,000 	$948	$100	$250
Large Home 3 bedrooms/2 bathrooms/1,800 Sq. Ft $200,000 	$1,517	$125	$325

+Property Taxes and PMI (Private Mortgage Insurance)

*Based on 30 year FHA (First Time Homebuyer) Loan with 3.5% down payment and 7.5% interest rate.

RENTAL APARTMENT	Monthly Rent	Renter's Insurance	Utilities
Live at Home Your Current Bedroom	$300		
1 Bedroom Apartment 1 bedroom 1 bathroom 600 Sq. Ft 	$850	$15	$45
2 Bedroom Apartment * 2 bedroom 1 bathroom 950 Sq. Ft 	$1400 *$700 if you have a roommate	$15	$60 *$30 if you have a roommate

Your Housing Choice

Rent or Mortgage _____

Insurance _____

Utilities _____

Roommate   Roommate's Name _____

                      Teacher Initials _____

Housing Total _____

To track your spending as you go, enter these numbers into your Monthly Budget Tracker on pg. 19.

FOOD

Food Directions

After finding the shelter of a place to live, your next adult spending choice is food. Budgeting for food involves making a plan for how much you will eat at home, how many times you plan to stop for coffee before work, and how often you plan to eat at restaurants, or have food delivered.

GROCERIES

Eating at home will almost always cost significantly less than eating at a restaurant or ordering delivery.

Over time, eating healthy home-cooked food will mean lower medical bills. To take the best advantage of the savings that eating at home affords, take some time to ask good cooks in your life for lessons and tips.

RESTAURANTS

Do you like to cook at home? If not, you may find yourself eating out more than you planned, which could break your budget. When you eat out, you're paying not only for the food but more for the convenience and atmosphere.

While the average cost of eating out changes significantly depending on the restaurant, most restaurants charge around five times more on the items they serve than if you bought the groceries yourself. This price increase is to cover the restaurants' overhead.

> *Overhead-* Ongoing expenses the business must pay to stay in business, such as employees' wages, advertising, utilities, and rent. These are expenses that are in addition to the cost of the raw materials needed to make the meal.

Be realistic in your choices. Many young adults try to save money by swearing never to eat out, but for many it is unrealistic to think you will only cook at home. Restaurants are not just about food; they are also about interacting with friends or taking advantage of the convenience to do other needed tasks. What if your co-workers go out to eat once a week; will you really stay in the office by yourself? Will you really bring your lunch to work every single day?

If it is possible that you will eat out some time during the month, then you must budget for it.

DRINKS

When planning your monthly food budget, many must plan for drinks also. Do you like coffee drinks? Would you rather drink a latte than a plain black coffee you make at home? Do you like an ice-cold fountain drink over a canned drink? These small drinks add up quickly in a budget so they must be planned for.

MAKE YOUR FOOD CHOICE

Review the expenses of food then choose the options that you think would work best for you. It is required for you to pick a budget for groceries but may also add à la carte from eating out and drinking options.

*If you chose to live at home, you still must purchase the required monthly groceries, it is not included in your rent. Even if you are not the one cooking it, you will still need to contribute to the high cost of groceries.

Food Options		Cost	Monthly Cost
Monthly Groceries for one person *Required*		$200	$200
Fast Food twice a week *Optional*		$10 x 8	$80
Take out or pizza delivery once a week *Optional*		$25 x 4	$100
Eat at a sit-down restaurant twice a month *Optional*		$30 x 2	$60

Coffee/Drink Options	Cost	Monthly Cost
Coffee House specialty drink twice a week	$4.50 x 8	$36
Coffee every day at home, 2 bags of coffee each month	$8 x 2	$16
Large Soft Drink three times a week	$2 x 12	$24

Your Food Choice

Groceries _____

Fast Food _____

Take-out _____

Restaurants _____

Coffee/Drinks _____

Food Total _____

To track your spending as you go, enter these numbers into your Monthly Budget Tracker on pg. 19.

TRANSPORTATION

Transportation Directions

You have food and shelter. Your next task is to determine how you will get to your job, grocery store, the doctor, etc. Think about the job you have chosen and the area where you would like to live when considering your mode of transportation.

MONTHLY PAYMENT

For each transportation choice you must record your monthly payment. In this workbook, monthly costs are based on sixty-month car loan with zero down payment and 4.5% interest rate. Some of you may want to pay cash for a vehicle in real life, and choose not to get a loan, but for simplicity of this exercise the monthly payment still indicates how much you need to budget to save for a car, even if you pay for it with cash.

Car loan- A loan that allows you to borrow money from a lender and use that money to purchase a car. You'll have to repay the loan in fixed installments over a set period, and interest will be charged on the money you borrow. Your credit score will affect your ability to get a car loan or good interest rate.

Car Lease- Type of auto financing that allows you to "rent" a car from a dealership for a certain length of time and/or number of miles. Leases often have lower monthly payments than a car loan, but instead of building equity in the car, at the end of the lease, you'll return the vehicle to the dealership.

GAS

Owning a vehicle has several hidden costs above your monthly payment. Considering how much gas you will need should inform what type of vehicle you buy.

Gas Mileage- the distance, measured in miles, that a car can travel for each gallon of fuel. Miles Per Gallon (MPG) is primary measurement of a car's fuel efficiency: The higher a car's MPG, the more fuel efficient it is.

AUTO INSURANCE

Auto insurance is not an option, almost every state requires you to pay for auto insurance. It covers damage to your vehicle and protects you financially if you're responsible for someone else's injuries or damages. Auto insurance can also pay for medical bills if you or your passengers are injured in an accident, or if you're hit by an uninsured or underinsured driver.

REGISTRATION

A vehicle registration officially states that a vehicle can be driven on public roads and connects a vehicle to both a state and an owner. Every state requires motor vehicles to be registered and titled with the state's department of motor vehicles. If you ever get pulled over by a police officer, they will ask for your registration to prove you are the owner of the vehicle you are driving. Registration fees, annually or bi-annually, vary significantly from state to state and type of vehicle. For this exercise we are establishing an annual fee of $120, which you will budget for each month.

CAR MAINTENANCE AND REPAIR

Purchasing a car also requires you to budget to pay for car repairs, which includes preventative maintenance and other repairs.

Preventative Car Maintenance includes oil changes, transmission flushes, brake pad replacement, etc. Regular maintenance can prevent larger more costly repairs down the road. For example, an oil change can cost $40 every three to six months, but if you have to replace your entire engine it would be closer to $5,000. With preventative maintenance, you can either pay a little now or pay a lot later.

PUBLIC TRANSPORTATION

Owning a vehicle comes with several hidden costs, so many people choose to use public transportation instead. This is only a viable option depending on your location and job. Not all areas have subways and buses.

An advantage of public transportation is you can be more productive on your commute. It is also good for the environment as you're releasing less pollution into the air. A disadvantage is that public transportation runs on its own schedule, not yours. It will take longer to wait for your bus, sit through multiple stops, and still must walk home depending on how close you live to a stop. This will add a few hours to your commute time.

BICYCLE

A bicycle may be the least expensive option but could be impractical depending on what type of job you have or where you live. Wearing a suit with a bike is difficult. If you work in a different city than where you live, the lack of bicycle lanes in the area, and weather conflicts, particularly in the winter and rainy seasons can make a bicycle an unrealistic option.

RIDE SHARING / TAXI

Using ride sharing, such as Uber or Lyft, or a Taxi can be practical if you work from home and do not plan to go out more than a few times a week. This option is different than a bus, as you can use these on your own schedule, but they are significantly more expensive. Depending on your area, a one-way ride can cost as much as half a tank of gas.

MAKE YOUR TRANSPORTATION CHOICE

Review the expenses of transportation, then choose the option that you think would work best for you. Please do not make a choice just because it is the cheapest. Really consider what your job and location will require. If you do choose a vehicle, you will need to factor in ALL the costs on your budget tracker.

VEHICLE	Monthly Payment	Auto	Gas	Auto Repair	Registration $120/year
Used Car* $7,000	$126	$50	$150	$200	$10
Used SUV* $10,000	$180	$50	$175	$200	$10
New Car+ $28,000	$448	$85	$125	$100	$10
New Pick-Up Truck+ $40,000	$640	$85	$200	$100	$10

*Used Car Based on 72 month Car Loan 0% down payment and Good Credit Score of 9% interest rate.

+New Car Based on 72 month Car Loan 0% down payment and Good Credit Score of 4% interest rate.

Other Methods of Transport	Monthly Cost
Bicycle	$10
Monthly Bus Pass	$50
Monthly Subway Pass	$75
Ride Sharing/Taxis $15 per ride/one way 2 rides 2 days a week	$240

Your Transportation Choice

Monthly Payment _____

Car Insurance _____

Gas _____

Auto Repair _____

Bus or Uber _____

Registration _____

Transportation Total _____

To track your spending as you go, enter these numbers into your **Monthly Budget Tracker on pg. 19.**

Health Directions

Health insurance is complicated and varies greatly depending on your needs and job. Think about your wants and needs, and then make the best choice based on your salary and your own personal health. If you have any special medical needs, like diabetes, allergies, or asthma, you might have to see the doctor more often, and you would want that covered by your insurance.

> _Health Coverage_- Legal entitlement to payment or reimbursement for your health care costs, generally under a contract with a health insurance company, a health plan offered in connection with your employment, or a government program like Medicare, Medicaid.

> _Premium_- The amount you pay for your health insurance every month

You only need to add your monthly premium costs to your budget, but it is important to understand that isn't your entire health cost. In addition to your premium, throughout the year adults face many other health care costs, including a deductible and co-payments. Lower monthly premiums mean higher deductibles.

> _Deductible_- A deductible is the amount you pay for health care services each year before your health insurance pays its portion of the cost of covered services.

> _Co-Payment_- A fixed amount ($30, for example) you pay for a covered health care service after you've paid your deductible.

It is suggested to save a small percentage of your income each month to pay for these types of health costs. Your employer may help you save for health costs, but we are not assuming that in this exercise.

EMPLOYER PROVIDED

Your job option designates if you have employer provided insurance or if you must buy from the marketplace.

> _Employer-Sponsored Health Insurance_ - Healthcare plan that employers provide for their workers and their dependents. The employer is responsible for choosing the plan and determining exactly what it covers. Health Insurance is naturally less expensive if an employer provides it because employers and employees typically share the cost of health insurance premiums.

MARKETPLACE

If your employer does not provide health insurance, you will need to shop for your own insurance. The Healthcare Marketplace is a service that helps people shop for and enroll in health insurance. There are a few different options for Healthcare Marketplaces.

The federal government operates the Health Insurance Marketplace ®, available at _HealthCare.gov_, for most states. Some states run their own Marketplaces.

DENTAL AND VISION

Dental and Vision are optional but depending on your needs could be a good investment. Do you wear glasses or contacts? Vision insurance will lower your costs of exams and replacement. Do you have braces or a retainer? The cost of braces without dental insurance is high. Dental insurance also covers preventive care which can save you money and pain later.

MAKE YOUR HEALTH CHOICE

Review the expenses of health insurance. If the job you have chosen has an employer provided health coverage, pick one of the Employer Health Plans. If your job has Marketplace health coverage, pick from one of the Marketplace options.

It is required for you to pick a health plan, but you do not have to pick dental or vision unless you think it best for you.

EMPLOYER Individual Health Plans	Deductible	Monthly Premium
Standard	$1200	$100
High Deductible Health Plan (HDHP)	$3000	$50

MARKETPLACE Individual Health Plans	Deductible	Monthly Premium
Bronze- Least helpful	$6,500	$350
Silver- Average coverage	$4500	$450
Gold- Most helpful if you have regular doctors' visits and prescriptions	$1500	$630

Optional Health Plans	Monthly Premium
Dental (optional)	$10
Vision (optional)	$13
Health Savings (optional)	$30 a month or more

Your Health Choice

Monthly Premium   _____
Vision   _____
Dental   _____
Health Savings   _____

Health Total   _____

To track your spending as you go, enter these numbers into your Monthly Budget Tracker on pg. 19.

ELECTRONICS

Electronics Directions

In today's connected world it is important to budget for a phone and internet plan. Determine your needs based on job, salary, and lifestyle.

CELL PHONE

Cell Phones can have a large price range. In the modern age, not having a phone is unrealistic. The cost of a cell phone can range dramatically depending on company and features. Some plans will give you a phone at a discount in exchange for signing a contract, which has advantages and disadvantages.

Cell Phone Contract- A legal commitment between a phone carrier and customer where the customer pays a single monthly fee for a fixed period of time (usually one-year or two-years). The drawback is if you are unhappy with your carrier you cannot change without paying a large fee to break the contract.

Prepaid Phone Plans- No contract monthly plans are when you pay upfront at the beginning of each month. This means there's no penalty for canceling or switching carriers. The downside is no discount on the cost of your phone and if you miss a payment your carrier will cut off your phone service.

INTERNET

Just like cell phones, in the modern age you need access to the internet.

Internet- The global system of interconnected computer networks that use the Internet protocol to link devices worldwide. Modem, routers, switches are needed to connect to internet servers.

Broadband- The cable that comes into your home and is plugged into a wireless router.

_Wi-Fi-_ WiFi stands for Wireless Fidelity. WiFi is a small network where smartphones, computers or other networkable devices are connected to each other or the internet wirelessly within a small range. Wi-Fi is the radio signal sent from a wireless internet router to a nearby device, which translates the signal into data you can see and use.

While there are a lot of opportunities to find Wi-Fi at stores and libraries, relying solely on free Wi-Fi is not feasible if your job requires internet access. Free Wi-Fi is limited to location and has slower upload and download speeds, which may hinder job related tasks. Many jobs require reliable internet access. Streaming Services also need the internet to work reliably.

Paying for Wi-fi also allows you to pick a cheaper cell phone plan with limited data. You can use your Wi-Fi instead of your phone data to stream movies and use apps.

MAKE YOUR ELECTRONICS CHOICE

Review the expenses of a phone and internet, then choose the options you think would work best for you. It is required to budget for the cost of the phone and your monthly plan. You must choose an internet plan if you have chosen any type of streaming services in your entertainment budgeting.

*If you choose to live at home, you do not need an Internet plan, it is covered in your rent. If you have a roommate, you can split the cost for the Internet.

Cell Phones	Cost of Phone	Monthly Plan
Smartphone with Cell Phone Contract National Cell Service Carrier Unlimited Data Plan	Included in your plan	$100
Smartphone with Prepaid Month to Month Plan Limited Data Plan	$25 a month ($300 phone)	$45

Internet/ Wi-Fi*	Monthly Cost
Basic Internet	$45
High Speed Internet	$80

Your Electronics Choice

Cell Phone _____

Monthly Plan _____

Internet _____

Electronics Total _____

To track your spending as you go, enter these numbers into your Monthly Budget Tracker on pg. 19.

PERSONAL CARE

Personal Care Directions

Personal items, such as clothing, grooming, and home goods are essential in life. Budgeting for the amount you will spend on personal care items prevents expensive shopping sprees and impulse purchases.

CLOTHING

Your clothing budget should match your career. An attorney will need to own suits for court, and you can expect to spend $400 to $800 on a basic suit. A nurse will need scrubs and good shoes since they are on their feet all day. Someone who works from home will only require a casual wardrobe.

PERSONAL GROOMING

Personal Grooming involves how you take care of your hair and body, including haircuts, makeup, shaving, lotions, etc. Men and boys may not use makeup but tend to need their hair cut more often than women. Consider your personal habits now, do you cut your hair at home or do you like it professionally done? Do you like name brand shampoo, toothpaste, or acne cream?

> *Toiletries*- Items used in washing and taking care of one's body, such as toothpaste, soap, shampoo, shaving cream, or cologne.

HOME GOODS

Home goods are the tangible and movable personal property placed in the rooms of a house. Home Goods are what you are going to sit and sleep on, art on your wall, and blankets on your bed. They are the dishes in your kitchen cabinets and pots you used to cook.

Home goods range in price depending on your needs and personal taste, but the expenses of these sizable items need to be planned for. Did you know a couch can cost between $300 and $3,000? A television is between $200 and $1,000. A mid-range mattress can cost $500-$1,500.

MAKE YOUR PERSONAL CARE CHOICES

You must make one clothing, one personal grooming, and one home goods choice. You might need to do a little research to discover the appropriate clothing for your career choice. If you live at home, you do not need to include a Home Goods choice.

Clothing	Description	Monthly Cost
Business Professional	This plan is for professionals in industries such as finance, law, government and Communications/Public Relations. Includes several suits, sport coats and slacks or dresses and pant suits with dress shirts and dress shoes. Includes casual wear.	$200
Business Casual	This plan is for employees in most offices. Contains much of the same as business professional, but without the suits. Still requires a jacket for important events or meetings. Includes casual wear.	$100
Casual	This plan is meant for some work-from-home positions, service industry jobs as well as contractors and construction workers. Consists of mostly collared shirts, tee shirts, shoes, shorts and pants. Includes non-work casual wear.	$50
Uniform	Includes several sets of uniforms and shoes for those in medical, firefighting, police, and maintenance career. Some uniforms require professional cleaning. Also includes casual wear.	$75

Home Goods	Description	Monthly Cost
Fine furniture	Pottery Barn, Crate and Barrel, Ethan Allen	$500
Ordinary furniture	TJ Maxx, Home Goods	$300
Discount, self-assembled	Costco, IKEA Walmart	$150
Second Hand & Thrift Store	Goodwill, Salvation Army, Garage Sales, Hand-Me-Downs	$50

Personal Grooming	Description	Monthly Cost
High-End	• Haircut & Styling every 6 weeks for women and every other week for men • Name-brand shampoo, makeup and shaving supplies • Manicures or Barbershop Shave • High End Toiletries	$150
Average	• Haircut every three to four months for women and once a month for men • Average shampoo, makeup, and shaving supplies • Average Toiletries	$50
Budget	• Basic Haircut every six to eight months • Bulk shampoo • No make-up • No special shaving supplies • Basic toiletries	$25

Your Personal Care Choice

PERSONAL

Clothing _____

Home Goods _____

Personal Grooming _____

Personal Total _____

To track your spending as you go, enter these numbers into your Monthly Budget Tracker on pg. 19.

EDUCATION

Education Directions

In general, the more education you have, the higher your overall income will be, but a lot depends on what you study and how much your schooling costs.

COLLEGE COSTS

The cost of colleges varies based on private versus public. This workbook provides average costs of attending college purely for informational purposes. You do not need to calculate your yearly costs, but it is helpful for you to see the total costs of higher education, not just monthly payments.

Along with tuition, you'll probably have to pay some other fees to enroll in and attend a college, such as technology and processing fees. Tuition and fees vary from college to college. Other college costs include room and board, books and supplies, transportation, and personal expenses.

Tuition- The price you pay for college classes.

Room and Board- On-campus college housing that is accompanied by a meal plan.

Public College- Higher education institutions that are also funded by state governments.

Private College- Higher education not funded by state government. Rely more heavily on student tuition fees, alumni donations, and endowments to fund their academic programs. Typically, private colleges have higher tuition fees than public colleges.

Financial Aid- Money given or lent to you to help you pay for college. Most full-time college students receive some form of financial aid.

- Grants & Scholarships- Free aid (otherwise known as "gift aid"), meaning they do not need to be paid back, making them the most sought-after options.
  - Grants are given based on financial need, while scholarships are merit-based and awarded to students based on their academic achievements, extracurricular activities, field of study, and more.
- Student Loans- Money for college that is not "free" and needs to be repaid, with substantial interest. Student loans have repayment terms as long as 20 years. Because the loan term is so much longer, lenders charge higher rates on student loans. Because of this structure, many pay off their student loans for most of their adult life.

Some of you may not get student loans in your real life, instead rely on family or scholarships. For the purpose of this exercise, we want you to still designate a monthly savings plan for education since statistically most of you will have to finance your own education. We have included the average costs students in America pay in student loans, remember this payment monthly is for up to 20 years after you graduate.

Education: Yearly Costs

Average cost of attending college	(including room and board)
Certificate at Community College	$2,250 (one year certificate)
2-year community college	$4,500 per year
4-year in-state college or university	$25,615 per year
4-year private college or university	$53,949 per year
Graduate school	• $140,000 for public Master's • $180,879 for private law school • $251,524 for public medical school • $402,444 for private medical school

CHOOSE YOUR MONTHLY EDUCATION COST

You must use the designated education level on your job option to pick your monthly payment. This should already be filled out on your Monthly Budget Tracker. If you need a bachelor's degree, you can decide if you want to go to a private or public college.

Degree	Average Monthly Payment
Doctoral Degree	$1200
Law School	$750
Post-Graduate Master's Degree	$700
4 Year Bachelors' Degree Private College	$550
4-year Bachelor's Degree Public State University	$350
2-year Associate's Degree State or Community College	$225
Certificate	$100

Your Education Choice
ELECTRONICS
Monthly Payment _____
Education Total _____

To track your spending as you go, enter these numbers into your Monthly Budget Tracker on pg. 19.

SAVINGS

Savings Directions

Savings means planning for the future through investment, saving for big goals, or investing in others. When you don't make a plan to save, you fall into the destructive cycle of living paycheck to paycheck. As of September 2022, 63% of Americans were living paycheck to paycheck, according to a Lending Club report.

> Living Paycheck to Paycheck- to spend all of the money from one paycheck before receiving the next paycheck

Saving for the future is a privilege. There are legitimate reasons someone may not be able to make more than their expenses, such as a health situation that doesn't allow them to work more/find a better paying job. There can also be an unequal access to education that does not allow advance in a better paying job.

Some people are *able* to make more than their basic needs, but not willing to restrain their spending on items that would be considered a "want". Many times they fall under the belief once you pay all your bills then any money leftover can be used for fun things, like vacations or restaurants.

If you are able to save, meaning your income is more than your basic needs, we highly encourage you to set aside money each month for retirement, savings goals, and giving.

RETIREMENT

Living Paycheck to Paycheck is dangerous because it leaves no plan for retirement.

> *Retire*- to withdraw from one's position or occupation : having concluded one's working or professional career

> *Investment*- An investment is an asset or item acquired with the goal of generating income or appreciation.

In the United Sates, the median retirement age is 64 and the median age of death is 73 years old. Without a retirement plan, what do you plan to live on during those 10 years? And if you live longer, then what?

Retirement savings is most effective when started early in life due to compound interest.

> *Compound Interest*- when you earn interest on both the money you've saved and the interest you earn.

To illustrate the importance of saving early, below are investing plans based on when a person starts saving $2000 a year/$167 a month at age 15, 25, 35, 45, & 55.

Age you begin investing $2,000 annually ($167/month)	Amount saved by age of 65
15	$615,512
25	$328,095
35	$167,603
45	$77,985
55	$27,943

SAVING GOALS

Living paycheck to paycheck is risky because it does not leave room to save a contingency fund for the unexpected.

Contingency Fund- a reserve of money set aside to cover possible unforeseen future expenses.

In several spending chapters we have designated that you save for extra items, like car repair, but the amount you saved is for regular maintenance. You will need new tires, oil changes, fluid checks. But what happens if your car engine completely stops working and you need a new car? Cars do not last forever. Saving for your next vehicle, or newer vehicle, is a smart budget plan.

You saw the short- and long-term benefits of owning a home versus renting. If you want to get out of giving your rent money to someone else by buying your own home, you will need to save up for a down payment. That money will not save itself; it must be intentionally designated.

While owning a home for 10 or more years is always a good financial choice in the long term, home repairs are one of the leading causes of busting your budget. If your refrigerator dies, you are the one responsible for buying a new one. Leak in the roof? You are paying for it.

We also save for expected costs throughout the year. Christmas and Birthdays are not an unexpected expense. The average American spends almost $1,000 on Christmas. You can choose how much you would like to save in your monthly budget based on your monthly income.

GIVING

When we factor in charitable giving, we are investing not only in others but in our own physical and mental health. Studies have proven that generosity can lower blood pressure, reduce anxiety, improve depression, and lower stress levels.

This workbook gives a few options to practice generosity.

Charitable Donations- A gift of money made to a nonprofit organization to help it accomplish its goals, for which the donor receives nothing of monetary value in return.

Nonprofit Organization - An organization that works to provide societal benefit and does not distribute profit to any private individuals.

Tithing- A tithe is a portion (usually 10%) of your income given as an offering to your local church. The word 'tithe' literally means tenth in Hebrew and many Christians and Jews practice it as part of their faith.

Community Service- A gift of time to a nonprofit organization to help it accomplish its goals, for which the donor receives nothing of monetary value in return.

MAKE YOUR SAVINGS CHOICES

Retirement- You can make a flat investment of $167 a month or calculate 3%, and up to 15% of your monthly earnings towards a retirement plan. Employers will sometimes match retirement savings, but we have not assumed that in this exercise.

Investment	Monthly Cost
Retirement Roth IRA	$167 a month or 3% to 15% of your monthly income

If you bought a home, you must save a full $100 a month for home repairs. You can save more if you choose. All other saving goals are optional, but we encourage you to strongly consider planning for your future.

Savings Goals		Monthly Cost
Home Repairs *Required for those who purchased a home in Housing Chapter*		$100+
Down Payment on a House *Optional*		Suggested goal of $100+
New Car *Optional*		Suggested goal of $100+
Gift Fund Christmas and Birthday Presents *Optional*		Suggested goal of $50+

Giving	Monthly Cost
Religious Tithe *Optional*	10% of *gross* income
Sponsor a Compassion Child or World Vision Water Ministry+ *Optional*	$40
4 Hours of Community Service *Optional*	$0

Your Savings Choice

Retirement	_____
Home Repair	_____
House Down Payment	_____
Save for New Car	_____
Gift Fund	_____
Giving	_____
Saving Total	_____

To track your spending as you go, enter these numbers into your Monthly Budget Tracker on pg. 19.

ENTERTAINMENT

Entertainment Directions

The entertainment budget category represents the "nice to have" services, including music, movies, videos, concerts, pets, and vacations. Entertainment has the most appealing options. These spending choices should always come last, after all your needs and savings are done. Your job is to think about your wants and needs, and then make the best choice based on your salary.

MOVIES AND MUSIC

Many people consume their movies and music through online streaming subscription. Subscription costs can seem small, like only $5 a month, but when you pay for many subscriptions, they add up very quickly.

> Streaming Service- a service that sends video, music, etc., over the internet so that people can watch or listen to it immediately rather than having to download it, or rather than having to watch or listen at a particular time when something is broadcasted or in a movie theater. Streaming cannot be used without an internet connection.

VACATIONS

Vacations are expensive and should be budgeted for ahead of time. No one wants to come home after a trip with regret, or the inability to pay their rent because they spent too much their vacation.
Putting aside a small amount each month for your vacation is the best way to ensure you don't go into debt during your vacation. The chart provides the total costs for each vacation option for you to see how expensive vacations are overall, but you will only use the Monthly Cost on your Monthly Budget Tracker.

PETS

Pets are wonderful companions in life but an expensive addition to any budget. Their constant needs, including regular and unexpected vet visits, must be budgeted for before taking on the responsibility of another life.

MAKE YOUR ENTERTAINMENT CHOICE

Review the expenses of entertainment, then choose the options that would work best for your salary and lifestyle. All items in entertainment are optional.

You may only get streaming service if you have also purchased an internet package in your electronics budget.

*If you choose to live at home, you do not need an Internet plan for streaming, it is covered in your rent.

Movies and Music	Monthly Cost
hulu Video Streaming service	$7
prime video Video Streaming service	$13
Disney+ Video Streaming service	$13
Spotify Music Streaming service	$10
audible Audiobook Streaming service	$18
hulu Disney+ ESPN+ Hulu + Disney + ESPN	$85
Gaming (consoles and new games)	$25
Concert or Sports Tickets ($84 once a year)	$7

Vacation	Monthly Cost
Visit Cancun, Mexico $2,160 for one person for one week	$180
Visit London, England $3,000 for one person for four nights	$250
Visit Chicago, Illinois $300 for one person for the one night	$25
$120 Includes gas, food, campsite for 2 days	$10

Pets	Monthly Cost
$1200 Includes shots, vet visits, & monthly food	$100
$840 Includes shots, vet visits, cat food, & litter	$70
$60 Includes tank, food, & filters	$5

Your Entertainment Choice

Movies & Music _____

Vacation _____

Pet Care _____

Entertainment Total _____

To track your spending as you go, enter these numbers into your Monthly Budget Tracker on pg. 19.

CHANCE

Chance Directions

Materials Needed: A set of dice

Budgeting includes planning for the unexpected. Cars break down, we drop our phones, laptops crash. Not all medical emergencies are covered by your insurance. No one is exempt from chance. Planning margin in your budget for the unexpected enables you to set aside money each month, which can prevent the unexpected turning into a budget buster.

To complete the change section, roll your dice two times:

1st roll: Roll the Dice, the sum of your dice is your first chance event.

2nd roll: Roll the Dice again, the sum of your dice is your second chance event.

2	Computer Crash -$420	LOSE -$35 a month
3	Work Bonus +$180	GAIN +$15 a month
4	Your wallet is stolen - $360	LOSE -$30 a month
5	Birthday Gift + $120	GAIN +$10 a month
6	Emergency Dental Appointment - $420	LOSE -$35 a month
7	Dropped your Smart Phone - $600	LOSE -$50 a month
8	Tax Return + $300	GAIN +$25 a month
9	Got the flu, missed several days of work -$420	LOSE -$35 a month
10	Speeding Ticket - $180	LOSE -$15 a month
11	Worked a part time job + $180	GAIN +$15 a month
12	Paid a bill late, incurred a fee - $120	LOSE -$10 a month

Your Chance Choice

Chance

Roll One   _____

Roll Two   _____

Chance Total   _____

To track your spending as you go, enter these numbers into your Monthly Budget Tracker on pg. 19.

Balance Your Budget

You have chosen all your monthly expenses, and it is time to balance your budget. Go back to your Budget Tracker on page 22 and add up all your expenses to determine if you have a balanced budget.

Balanced Budget- Occurs when income is equal to or greater than total expenses, a budget with no deficit or surplus.

DEFECIT– YOU SPENT TOO MUCH MONEY

If you have added all your expenses and have spent more money than your monthly income, you have a budget deficit.

Budget Deficit- Occurs when spending is more than your income.

If you have a budget deficit, first revisit the "Wants" chapters of Electronics and Entertainment to make different choices. You can then revisit extra food spending, like not eating out as much. Do not reduce essentials like housing and transportation to your place of employment without first reducing non-essential spending.

SURPLUS– YOU HAVE MONEY LEFT OVER

If you have added all your expenses and have money left over, you have a budget surplus.

Budget Surplus- Occurs when spending is less than your income, you make more money than you spent.

Some assume a budget surplus is ideal, but studies have shown when you do not budget all your money you tend to spend it faster, which eventually leads to a deficit. A surplus can lead to impulse purchases thinking, "I have a little extra, I can afford it."

If you have a surplus, please allocate it to a specific savings goal. Keeping a savings goal is a proven method to prevent impulse spending.

Unit III:

Student Reflection

1. How did you decide which job to choose? (you may choose more than one)

- ☐ I know someone who does this for a living.
- ☐ Something I always wanted to do.
- ☐ I thought the job would pay a lot of money.
- ☐ I thought it was a job that would always be in demand and had growth opportunities.
- ☐ I used the career surveys from this book.
- ☐ I did not complete a career survey and randomly picked a job that sounded ok.

2. What was the most helpful information about managing money that you learned in this workbook?

_____

_____

_____

_____

_____

_____

3. How has this workbook changed the way you plan to save or spend money?

_____

_____

_____

_____

_____

4. What did you enjoy most about the workbook?

_____

_____

_____

_____

_____

_____

5. What surprised you most about making a budget?

_____
_____
_____
_____
_____
_____

6. What was the most difficult part of the making a budget (you may choose more than one)

☐ Understanding what my options were
☐ Tracking whether or not I was overspending
☐ Deciding on the best choices for my income
☐ Spending more money than I had in my income
☐ Other:

_____
_____
_____

7. Did this workbook affect your plans for a job, if so how??

_____
_____
_____
_____
_____
_____

Unit IV:

BUDGETING WITH
LOCAL COST OF LIVING

This is an optional exercise and will need more assistance from your teacher and other adults in your life to complete.

Congratulations on completing a real-life budget based on real life numbers! Hopefully, you now understand a little better about all the different decisions in life.

The salaries and prices in this book are based on living in the most populated areas of the United States, the South and the Midwest. You may not live in those areas, or you do but your region differs. Cost of living is different depending on where you live.

> *Cost of Living-* The average cost of all basic necessities including food, housing, utilities, transportation, clothing and health care expenses.

The cost of food, transportation, and rents vary greatly depending on where you choose to live. For example, living in New York City will have a different cost of living than living in a small farming community in the Midwest. Housing is generally more expensive in urban cities like New York, so it will cost more to live there. The good news is your pay will also vary depending on where you live. As an adult it will be important to pick a job that matches the cost of living where you plan to stay.

1. Pick a job with local Entry Salary

After you've completed your first practice budget, you can complete a Monthly Budget Tracker using local entry level salaries and local cost of living.

identify the local entry level salary for your chosen profession and cost of living for basic needs. Use the job you chose for the workbook to research local salaries or pick another job title. When searching you must search *Entry Level Salary.* You will not enter the working field at the top of the pay scale.

Your Job Choice

Career	
Yearly Salary	
Degree Needed	
Health Benefits (employer provided or not)	

2. Determine Your Monthly Income using that salary

You have chosen your job, now you need to determine what you really have to spend each month by again figuring out your taxes. A reminder of these terms:

Income- Money received, especially on a regular basis, for work or through investments.

Gross Income- The sum of all wages and earnings before any taxes are taken out.

Net Income/Take Home Pay- Net income is the gross income minus taxes. Net Income is also known as "take hone pay" because it is what you take home after your employer takes taxes out of your paycheck. If you are self-employed, your check will be whole, but you will have to put aside money to pay taxes at a later date.

Taxes- A mandatory payment or charge collected by local, state, and federal governments from individuals or businesses to cover the costs of general government services, goods, and activities. Taxes pay for government services, like fire departments, road repair, police, and libraries.

Every state has a different tax system, but every person has to factor in federal taxes to their monthly budget.

Income Planning & Taxes Worksheet

Occupation:

Yearly Salary (Gross Income):

Education Level Needed:

Yearly Take Home Pay (Net Income):

Divide your income into the segments of the tax bracket. Calculate your taxes using sample below.

Tax bracket (based on Annual Salary)	Tax Rate	Your Income	Taxes
The first $11,000	10%		
The next $11,000 – $45,000	12%		
The next $45,00– $95,000	22%		
The next $95,00– $180,000	24%		
The next $180,000 – $230,000	32%		
The next $230,000 – $575,000	35%		
Over $575,000	37%		
	TOTAL		

SAMPLE *So, if you earn $65,000, your federal taxes will look like this:*

Tax bracket (based on Annual Salary)	Tax Rate	Your Income	Taxes
The first $11,000	10%	$11,000	x .10= $1,100
The next $11,000 to $45,000	12%	$34,000	x .12= $4,080
The next $45,000 to $95,000	22%	$20,000	x .22= $4,400
		$65,000	$9,580 Total Taxes

Subtract Your total taxes from your Yearly Salary to get your Yearly Take-Home Pay

_____ - _____ = _____

   Yearly Salary   Total Taxes   Yearly Take-Home Pay

Monthly Net Income (Take Home Pay)

   Divide your Yearly Take Home Pay by 12 = _____

                               Monthly Take Home Pay

                     (Money you have to spend in a month)

3. Complete a budget based on your local cost of living

When searching local cost of living, look for expenses that are based on a one income household, without children. As your expenses grow with age, your incomes will hopefully grow accordingly. Don't forget to search if benefits are included.

You can find cost of living prices by:

1. Asking friends and family their costs of living
2. Internet research.

Resources for Local Prices

Job Options/Income

- www.glassdoor.com
- www.indeed.com
- www.payscale.com

Housing

- www.trulia.com
- www.trulia.com/mortgage-payment-calculator/
- www.apartments.com

Health

- www.investopedia.com/how-much-does-health-insurance-cost-4774184
- www.ehealthinsurance.com/resources/individual-and-family/how-much-does-individual-health-insurance-cost

Transportation

- www.kbb.com
- www.newsnationnow.com/business/your-money/gas-costs-hundreds-more-for-average-american/www.cars.com/car-loan-calculator/
- www.moneygeek.com/insurance/auto/cheapest-liability-only-car-insurance/

Education

- https://educationdata.org/average-cost-of-college
- https://educationdata.org/average-graduate-student-loan-debt
- https://educationdata.org/average-debt-for-a-bachelors-degree
- https://educationdata.org/average-student-loan-payment

Monthly Budget Tracker

HOUSING

Rent or Mortgage _____

Insurance _____

Utilities _____

Roommate   *Roommate Initials* _____

              Teacher Initials _____

Housing Total _____

TRANSPORATION

Monthly Payment _____

Car Insurance _____

Gas _____

Auto Repair _____

Bus or Uber _____

Transportation Total _____

FOOD

Groceries _____

Fast Food _____

Take-out _____

Restaurants _____

Coffee/Drinks _____

Food Total _____

HEALTH

Monthly Premium _____

Vision _____

Dental _____

Health Total _____

PERSONAL

Clothing _____

Home Goods _____

Personal Grooming _____

Personal Total _____

EDUCATION

Monthly Payment _____

Education Total _____

Career	
Yearly Salary	
Degree Needed	
Health Benefits	
Monthly Take-Home Pay	

WANTS

ELECTRONICS

Cell Phone _____

Internet _____

Electronics Total _____

ENTERTAINMENT

Movies & Music _____

Vacation _____

Pet Care _____

Entertainment Total _____

SAVING

SAVINGS

Retirement _____

Home Repair _____

House Down Payment _____

Save for New Car _____

Gift Fund _____

Give to Charity _____

Saving Total _____

CHANCE

CHANCE

Roll One _____

Roll Two _____

Chance Total _____

END OF MONTH BALANCE: _____

TEACHER INITIALS: _____

Monthly Budget Tracker

HOUSING

Rent or Mortgage _____

Insurance _____

Utilities _____

Roommate *Roommate Initials* _____

Teacher Initials _____

Housing Total _____

TRANSPORATION

Monthly Payment _____

Car Insurance _____

Gas _____

Auto Repair _____

Bus or Uber _____

Transportation Total _____

FOOD

Groceries _____

Fast Food _____

Take-out _____

Restaurants _____

Coffee/Drinks _____

Food Total _____

HEALTH

Monthly Premium _____

Vision _____

Dental _____

Health Total _____

PERSONAL

Clothing _____

Home Goods _____

Personal Grooming _____

Personal Total _____

EDUCATION

Monthly Payment _____

Education Total _____

N E E D S

Career	
Yearly Salary	
Degree Needed	
Health Benefits	
Monthly Take-Home Pay	

ELECTRONICS

Cell Phone _____

Internet _____

Electronics Total _____

ENTERTAINMENT

Movies & Music _____

Vacation _____

Pet Care _____

Entertainment Total _____

W A N T S

SAVINGS

Retirement _____

Home Repair _____

House Down Payment _____

Save for New Car _____

Gift Fund _____

Give to Charity _____

Saving Total _____

S A V I N G

CHANCE

Roll One _____

Roll Two _____

Chance Total _____

C H A N C E

END OF MONTH BALANCE: _____

TEACHER INITIALS: _____

Monthly Budget Tracker

NEEDS

HOUSING
Rent or Mortgage ____________
Insurance ____________
Utilities ____________
Roommate *Roommate Initials* ______
Teacher Initials ______
Housing Total ____________

TRANSPORATION
Monthly Payment ____________
Car Insurance ____________
Gas ____________
Auto Repair ____________
Bus or Uber ____________
Transportation Total ____________

FOOD
Groceries ____________
Fast Food ____________
Take-out ____________
Restaurants ____________
Coffee/Drinks ____________
Food Total ____________

HEALTH
Monthly Premium ____________
Vision ____________
Dental ____________
Health Total ____________

PERSONAL
Clothing ____________
Home Goods ____________
Personal Grooming ____________
Personal Total ____________

EDUCATION
Monthly Payment ____________
Education Total ____________

Career	
Yearly Salary	
Degree Needed	
Health Benefits	
Monthly Take-Home Pay	

WANTS

ELECTRONICS
Cell Phone ____________
Internet ____________
Electronics Total ____________

ENTERTAINMENT
Movies & Music ____________
Vacation ____________
Pet Care ____________
Entertainment Total ____________

SAVING

SAVINGS
Retirement ____________
Home Repair ____________
House Down Payment____________
Save for New Car ____________
Gift Fund ____________
Give to Charity ____________
Saving Total ____________

CHANCE

CHANCE
Roll One ____________
Roll Two ____________
Chance Total ____________

END OF MONTH BALANCE: ____________
TEACHER INITIALS: ____________

ABOUT THE AUTHOR

Robyn Joyner has always loved children's literature and teaching.
She has a degree in Early Childhood and is currently a homeschool mother and writer.
She resides in Northern Indiana with her husband and twin sons.

Find more handwriting and workbooks

www.LearningCursive.org

Homeschool Blog at

www.LeadingThemToTheRock.com

Follow on Facebook

@totherockhomeschool